D1144992

THE GLOUCESTERSHIRE AND WARWICKSHIRE RAILWAY

MALCOLM RANIERI

HALSGROVE

First published in Great Britain in 2010

Copyright © Malcolm Ranieri 2010

All rights reserved. No part of this publication may be reproduced,
stored in a retrieval system, or transmitted in any form or by any
means without the prior permission of the copyright holder.

British Library Cataloguing-in-Publication Data
A CIP record for this title is available from the British Library

ISBN 978 1 84114 813 7

HALSGROVE
Halsgrove House,
Ryelands Industrial Estate,
Bagley Road, Wellington, Somerset TA21 9PZ
Tel: 01823 653777   Fax: 01823 216796
email: sales@halsgrove.com

Part of the Halsgrove group of companies.
Information on all Halsgrove titles is available at: www.halsgrove.com

Printed and bound in China by Toppan Leefung Printing Ltd

Introduction

The Gloucestershire and Warwickshire Railway runs from Toddington to Cheltenham Race Course, a distance of ten miles, through glorious Cotswold scenery. Whilst the railway currently personifies a Great Western branch line, before closure in Great Western and British Railways hands it was an important main line link from the Midlands to the South West. Its most famous train was "The Cornishman" which ran from Wolverhampton to Penzanze, from 1952 to 1962.

The original 1859 branch from Stratford upon Avon to Honeybourne was opened by the Oxford, Worcester and Wolverhampton Railway (OWW), colloquially known as the"Old, Worse and Worse". It was another forty years before the Great Western Railway, having swallowed up the OWW obtained an Act for a high speed line between Honeybourne and Cheltenham that they officially named the Cheltenham & Honeybourne line. The route opened in stages, finally being completed on 1 August, 1906, entering Cheltenham at Lansdowne Junction. Stratford upon Avon to Tysley was opened in 1908, giving the Great Western Railway an important strategic through route from the Midlands to the West Country. Gradual withdrawal of timetabled services took place through the 1960s, the last to go being the Leamington to Worcester services in May, 1969. Thereafter the only passenger trains using the line were diversions for engineering purposes and some race trains between Lansdowne Junction and Cheltenham Race Course. The ultimate blow came when a freight train derailed in August, 1976 at Winchcombe. Official closure south of Honeybourne was on 1 November, 1976. The Long Marston to Stratford upon Avon line was closed at this time, although a single line was retained for the Ministry of Defence between Honeybourne and Long Marston, as it is today.

Originally the preservation society was formed in 1976 to prevent closure of the line, or acquire it for private running. This did not stop the line being lifted in 1979. However, two years later in 1981 the current operating society, the Gloucestershire Warwickshire Steam Railway Plc, was incorporated to purchase the buildings that remained and the trackbed. The Light Railway Order was made on 24 December, 1983, an excellent Christmas present, and the line from Broadway to the outskirts of Cheltenham was acquired in February, 1984.

Since that time and with a completely volunteer workforce, as it is today, and a quite tremendous effort on their part, the current railway opened in stages in the 1980s from Toddington Station to firstly the Yard and then Hayles Abbey Halt, on to Winchcombe Station, where the original being demolished, was replaced by the re-erected brick-by-brick Monmouth Troy Station. Winchcombe Station should perhaps be rightly called Winchcombe Road as the town is a mile or so away, or Greet the village in which it is located. The next extension was in 1990 to a point south of the village of Gretton, and then gradually through the 1990s to the village of Far Stanley and Gotherington, finally in 2003 to Cheltenham Race Course Station. The railway's stated aim has always been to reach Stratford upon Avon, and the next stage of this long-term plan is north from Toddington Station to firstly Laverton Halt, and then Broadway a distance of 5 miles, where a new station is to be erected on the site of the old station, which has been completely demolished.

The route, currently all in Gloucestershire, starts from Toddington Station to the former Halt of Hayles Abbey, closed in 1960, running mostly on embankments above the fields, passing the village of Didbrook, where an original Cruck cottage can be seen. Hailes Abbey, spelt differently from the named halt, was founded in 1245 by Richard, Earl of Cornwall, and settled by Cistercian monks, finally succumbing to the infamous Dissolution of the Monasteries in the reign of King Henry VIII, in 1539, one of the last to do so. The ruins are in the care of the National Trust and English Heritage. Next to the ruins is the 1175-built Hailes Church which has some fine medieval wall paintings. The railway was built by the Great Western Railway to a maximum gradient of 1 in 108 and radius of curves set at half a mile, so therefore fierce gradients do not feature, and the line climbs gently from Toddington Station southwards to a plateau at Gretton Halt then slowly downhill to Cheltenham Race Course Station. The northbound gradients are the heaviest though nowhere does it exceed 1 in 150 from Bishops Cleeve to Gotherington. From Hayles Abbey Halt the line passes under a minor road bridge, which goes to Hailes Abbey and forks over Salters Hill, in low cuttings and onto the locally-named Defford Straight. The line then proceeds to the so-called Chicken Curve, because of a now defunct chicken farm whose buildings are seen adjacent to and below the line, where it crosses the B4632 on an overbridge and enters Winchcombe Yard. In the yard carriages, wagons and other machinery are stored, and here the railway's Carriage and Wagon Department have their depot in the old Goods Shed, the only original building remaining at Winchcombe Station when acquired. Overlooking the line is the escarpment of Salters Hill where the long distance Cotswold and Gloucester Ways footpaths meet. The views of the railway, the Vale of Evesham and towards the Malverns are quite outstanding from Salters Hill.

From Winchcombe Station the line goes underneath the road to Winchcombe Town, past the old Stationmaster's House, now a Bed and Breakfast establishment, and through a wide cutting to the northern portal of Greet Tunnel, which at 693 yards, is the second longest in preservation. The tunnel curves in the middle section, not allowing light to enter the whole length. The line then heads towards Gretton Village from the southern portal of Greet Tunnel in cuttings and on embankments, passing above the village and the previous Gretton Halt, like Hayles Abbey also closed in March, 1960, and over the road by the village church towards Far Stanley and Stanley Pontlarge. This was the hamlet where the famous author and preservasionist, L.T.C. Rolt lived at one stage. The next village passed is Dixton with a wide cutting and overbridge on a minor road to Alstone; the Prescott Hill Climb and the Bugatti Owners Club is based a few yards from the railway. Fine views can be seen from the train beyond Greet Tunnel especially on the western side towards Worcestershire and Herefordshire. Gotherington Station is privately owned, and the railway has built a halt on the opposite platform, used by walkers accessing the many footpaths which cross the Cotswold Hills. From here the train passes the new signalbox, not yet commissioned, and emerges beyond the village at Manor Farm Lane where the embankment takes the train to Bishops Cleeve. The station at Bishops Cleeve is now completely obliterated, but this was where the trains on major race days at Cheltenham Race Course were stabled, though difficult to imagine now. Across the only foot crossing on the line in the village of Bishops Cleeve, and through into open countryside, the views open out on to Cleeve Hill and the village of Southam on the outskirts of Cheltenham. The line enters the Race Course under Southam roadbridge and runs along the embankment which has been recently stabilised due to slips, into the Race Course Station.

Cheltenham Race Course Station, restored to a very high standard from derelict condition by the local supporters group, sits above the line on the edge of the Race Course. This was not open on normal operating days, and only used for race trains. The run round loop heads towards Cheltenham via Hunting Butts Tunnel and is currently the end of the line.

The railway's aim to re-open in the short-term to Broadway, north of Toddington Station, will mean crossing the impressive Stanway Viaduct, a 15 arch, 210 yard viaduct. When it was being built in November, 1903, number ten arch collapsed with fatalities. The track is lightly laid to Laverton Halt, also one of the March, 1960 closures, some two miles out of Toddington, where a railway bridge is to be re-instated over a minor road to Wormington village. Onwards over the fields to Broadway, where the station, run round, etc will have to be rebuilt, this extension will add a further five miles to the line.

Toddington is the headquarters of the railway where the locomotive sheds and engineering facilities are based and engines stabled. Winchcombe is the base for Carriage and Wagon. For operating purposes the railway has had to rely in the main on visiting engines, though currently 9F no 92203 "Black Prince" belonging to the artist, David Shepherd, OBE, is permanently stabled at the railway, as is the group-owned GWR Hall class no 7903 "Foremarke Hall" and the National Railway Museum's GWR City class no 3440 "City of Truro", arguably the first railway steam engine to exceed 100mph. Several engines owned by groups based at the railway are subject to long-term restoration. Among those engines expected to steam for the first time in many years shortly are the LMS and Turkish State Railway 8F no 8274, owned by the Churchill 8F locomotive Co; the 1905 (oldest preserved GWR locomotive) 28XX Heavy Goods Engine no 2807, owned by the Cotswold Steam Preservation Society; and the 1941 SR Merchant Navy Class no 35006 "Peninsular & Oriental S.N.Co.", owned by the P & O Society.

At Toddington Station situated on the edge of the car park is the second Toddington Station, which is the booking office for the North Gloucestershire Railway. This two foot gauge railway runs from Toddington southwards to their headquarters and second station on the line, where their fleet of locomotives, maintenance facilities, and memorabilia collection are situated, and then onwards to Didbrook paralleling the standard gauge line, approximately half a mile in length. This railway was formed from the Dowty Railway Preservation Society, which began in 1962, and restored both standard and narrow gauge stock on a site at Ashchurch next to the Dowty factory, and also ran trains on a circular track. Because of site closure the group re-located to Toddington from 1982 onwards, changed their name to the North Gloucestershire Railway and the members concentrated on two foot gauge, running a service on selected days from 1990.

The Stratford upon Avon and Broadway Railway Society was formed in 1995 with the aim of ensuring the future of the railway between those two places, and have a base at Long Marston, the former MOD Camp. Beyond Broadway the trackbed has been purchased (in 1998) by Sustrans, the National Cycle Network, with a view to opening the route beyond the trackbed from Stratford to Long Marston which is already a cycle route, to accommodate both railway and cycle path, though this lies very much in the future.

I have been a member and working volunteer, a Duty Stationmaster, for many years at the railway and watched it grow from virtually derelict condition to its current status in the top ten of the country's preserved railways, and a very fine tourist attraction in the Cotswolds. All this done by volunteers, an outstanding achievement, and which carries on. I dedicate this book to my fellow volunteers, past and present.

Malcolm Ranieri, FRPS

GWR 14XX no 1450 stands at Platform 2 at Toddington
Station with its auto-trailer coach awaiting her turn of duty.

On a misty day with the sun breaking through, GWR Heavy Goods Engine no 2857 brings a freight train south from Broadway into Platform 1 at Toddington Station.

GWR 14XX no 1450 stands at night underneath the
B4077 roadbridge at the north end of Toddington Station.

GWR Hall Class no 6990 "Witherslack Hall" brings a
freight train north through Platform 1 at Toddington Station.

GWR 14XX 1450 stands at night at Platform 2 at Toddington Station
with a branch line train, while the crew rest on the bench.

LMS Jinty no 47383 is photographed at night
waiting at Platform 1 at Toddington Station.

GWR Prairie Class no 4160 awaits her turn of duty on Platform 1 at Toddington Station.

In the early days of preservation the Gloucestershire and Warwickshire Railway at times used industrial locomotives to run the service. Here Peckett 0-4-0ST "Byfield" awaits departure.

A general winter scene at Toddington Station photographed
from the overbridge at Santa Special time in December.

Two GWR Hall Class locomotives stand at night at the south end
of Toddington Station, 6960 "Raveningham Hall" and 6990 "Witherslack Hall".

A recent Gala scene with Midland Railway 4F no 44422 with its freight train standing at Platform 2 at Toddington Station.

On the same Gala day, two visiting engines await duty: 4F no 44422 and SR West Country Light Pacific no 34007 "Wadebridge".

GWR 14XX no 1450 with its auto-trailer coach stands in the bay platform with Toddington Station in the background.

GWR Heavy Goods Engine no 2857 with its freight train moves from Platform 2 to take water at the tower.

Above:
GWR Pannier no 6412 departs Toddington Station
in the late afternoon with a passenger train.

Right:
GWR City Class no 3440 "City of Truro" takes a freight train past Didbrook village.

The railway holds a Vintage Gala in October most years.
The 1908 Robey Traction Engine "Pride of the Walk" poses at night.

A general view of Toddington Station taken from the signalbox. GWR Prairie no 5542 is about to back onto her train, with artist David Shepherd's BR 9F no 92203 on the shed line.

GWR Pannier no 9682 departs Toddington silhouetted against the setting sun with a winter special.

Industrial locomotive "Robert Nelson No.4" departs Toddington into the setting sun.

GWR Pannier no 9682 approaches Didbrook passing a colourful field of oil seed rape.

LMS Jinty no 47383 crosses the roadbridge over a minor road to the village of Didbrook with the last train of the day.

Above:
GWR Hall Class no 7903 "Foremarke Hall" approaches
the village of Didbrook northbound from Hayles Abbey.

Right:
An original stalwart of the steam fleet, now under restoration,
GWR Hall Class no 6960 "Raveningham Hall"
pulls its train round the curve at Didbrook.

GWR Hall Class no 4920 "Dumbleton Hall" thunders past the Toddington signalbox.
Dumbleton Hall is a local estate, a few miles from the railway, now a hotel.

A recent Gala visitor SR Lord Nelson Class no E850 "Lord Nelson" is on a freight train and passes Didbrook.

GWR Prairie no 5542 passes the site of some hard work by the clearance gang on the embankment at Didbrook.

GWR Prairie no 5542 approaches the houses at Didbrook passing over the minor road to the village.

Above:
A welcome visitor to the railway was the venerable Great Eastern Railway J15 no 65462
from the North Norfolk Railway. Here she is in charge of a freight train on Didbrook embankment.

Left:
GWR Hall Class no 6960 "Raveningham Hall" is framed in the branches
of an attractive tree in fields next to the railway at Didbrook.

The epitome of Great Western elegance, City Class no 3440 "City of Truro" takes her train past Didbrook. 3440 is on long term loan to the railway from the National Railway Museum.

GWR Prairie no 5542 is photographed side on to emphasize the auto-trailer coach in Great Western colours of chocolate and cream.

The Great Western Society's Heavy Goods Engine 28XX no 3822, doing what it was built to do, as it takes a freight train past Didbrook.

A very welcome visitor to the railway was the National Railway Museum's LNER V2 Class no 4771 "Green Arrow", a regular main line performer before her boiler certificate expired, here blasting past Didbrook.

Industrial Hunslet no 2409 "King George" 0-6-0ST is framed by a tree in the adjoining field to the embankment at Didbrook.

The J15 and freight are back-lit by the winter sun passing Didbrook.

GWR Hall Class no 4920 "Dumbleton Hall" is silhouetted against the setting
sun at Didbrook as it takes the last train of the day back to Toddington.

Midland Railway 4F no 44422 is on a freight train as it is silhouetted
against the bright sky; the sun can just be seen in the smoke.

GWR Hall Class no 6960 "Raveningham Hall" is an impressive sight as she approaches Hayles Abbey with the May blossom in evidence behind the locomotive.

This position was not enhanced by the power lines which now parallel the railway here, but the public footpath in the foreground makes this a regular place to watch the trains. 9F no 92203 "Black Prince", a resident engine, passes with the first train of the day.

Above:
GWR Heavy Goods Tank Engine no 5619 also approaches
Hayles Abbey past the saturated fields after winter rain.

Right:
This is the site of Hayles Abbey Halt, which never saw
much use and was closed in March, 1960. The rose bay willow
herb here is just coming into flower as Pannier no 7752 passes.

GWR Prairie no 5526, a recent visitor, passes the colourful
oil seed rape field next to the Hayles Abbey Halt site.

The last train of the day is pulled by 6960 "Raveningham Hall" and passes
the site of Hayles Abbey Halt with the Cotswold Hills as a backdrop.

Hayles Abbey Halt site sees GWR 14XX class no 1450 with auto-trailer coach take the late-afternoon train down the line.

The Gloucestershire and Warwickshire Railway has a large fleet of classic
modern traction, which besides the Diesel Galas, also work trains in certain
timetables throughout the year. Here Railfreight 47 no 47376 takes
over from the steam to work the last train of the day.

GWR 14XX no 1450 works her train under the minor road bridge which goes to the ancient monument of Hailes Abbey, a National Trust property; the road also leads over Salters Hill.

The minor road bridge is also passed by GWR Prairie Tank no 4566,
visiting the railway from its base on the Severn Valley Railway.

The auto-trailer coach is being driven towards Toddington at the site of Hayles Abbey Halt with 5542 supplying the power.

GWR Heavy Goods Tank Engine no 4247 with, appropriately enough, a freight train approaching the site of Hayles Abbey Halt.

Above:
GWR Pannier no 9681 takes the chocolate and cream coach set towards Toddington.

Left:
With back-lit storm lighting Jinty no 47383 approaches Hayles Abbey Halt site with a short freight train.

Approaching the so-called Defford Straight on its way to Winchcombe is
4920 "Dumbleton Hall" on a freight train with autumn colours in evidence.

GWR no 3440 "City of Truro" makes a fine sight as she approaches the Defford Straight.

GWR Manor Class 7822 "Foxcote Manor" takes the maroon set of coaches towards Winchcombe.

An unusual pairing is GWR 5619 and Midland 4F no 44422, though both are freight engines, here seen at a recent Gala on Defford Straight.

Above:
The J15 no 65462 works a two coach passenger train
passing the autumn colours on Defford Straight.

Right:
The J15 takes a short freight train towards Winchcombe
and is framed in a tree on the cutting edge.

Some spectacular views can be had of the surrounding Gloucestershire and Worcestershire countryside from Salters Hill. Here 7903 " Foremarke Hall" heads towards Toddington with the Vale of Evesham in the background.

From Salters Hill the train can be followed all the way from Winchcombe to Toddington and here 7903 "Foremarke Hall" makes for Hayles Abbey, the whole countryside sunlit.

Above:
3440 "City of Truro" approaches Winchcombe from Toddington
at the start of the location known as Chicken Curve.

Left:
From Salters Hill, and where the Cotswold and Gloucester Way
footpaths meet, the station at Toddington can just be seen in
the distance as 7903 "Foremarke Hall" approaches Hayles Abbey.

Above:
Just out of Winchcombe Station and Yards 9F 92203 "Black Prince" rounds Chicken Curve, so called because
of the buildings next to the embankment which were once a chicken farm, now industrial units, in a very wintry scene.

Right:
Another winter scene taken from Salters Hill with 9F 92203 "Black Prince" heading
towards Toddington with the village of Greet in the background.

Frost is melting as 7903 "Foremarke Hall" takes the first train of the day
northbound from Winchcombe to Toddington at Chicken Curve.

Another Great Western visitor 2251 Class no 3205 works a short freight around Chicken Curve picking up the back lighting at the end of the day.

Above:
In the same location, also a freight, this time
with Jinty no 47383 at Chicken Curve.

Right:
A winter scene from Salters Hill, but without the snow
as 7903 "Foremarke Hall" departs Winchcombe.

Above:
Closer to the Curve, GWR Prairie class no 4160 approaches the distant signal for Winchcombe with a passenger train composed of chocolate and cream liveried coaches.

Left:
In the autumn 7903 " Foremarke Hall" rounds Chicken Curve from Salters Hill. The Malverns can just be seen in the far background.

GWR Prairie no 5542 rounds the Curve with the auto-trailer and coach.

Visitor to a recent Gala, SR West Country Light Pacific no 34007 "Wadebridge"
also pulls her freight train around the Curve heading for Toddington.

Above:
GWR Pannier 9681 in the spring passes the blossom at Chicken Curve.

Right:
LMS Jubilee Class no 45596 "Bahamas" approaches Winchcombe Yards carrying a replica
'The Devonian' headboard and reporting number 1M37. This train ran
from the West Riding of Yorkshire to the Devon Coast.

Above:
In the same position as the Jubilee, GWR Hall Class no 6960
"Raveningham Hall" puts on a fine show as she heads for Winchcombe.

Right:
At Winchcombe, GWR no 4920 "Dumbleton Hall" catches the light at the end of the day.

Above:
GWR Pannier no 7752 crosses the B4632 taken from
the Winchcombe Town side of the railway bridge.

Left:
A GWR Prairie is silhouetted against the bright sky as she crosses the B4632
railway bridge, and into the Yards at Winchcombe Station.

GWR Pannier 6412 runs through Winchcombe Station. The station which is actually in the village of
Greet and should perhaps be called Winchcombe Road, is not original: Monmouth (Troy) Station was dismantled
brick-by-brick and re-assembled here. The Carriage and Wagon Sheds can be seen in the background as can Salters Hill.

GWR Hall Class 7903 "Foremarke Hall" works her way through Platform 2 at Winchcombe Station heading for Toddington.

SR Schools Class 30928 "Stowe", re-numbered and re-named sister engine 30925 "Cheltenham" especially
for the opening of Cheltenham Race Course Station in 2003, runs through Winchcombe Station.

GER J15 no 65462 simmers away on Platform 2 at Winchcombe Station.

Above:
GWR 2251 Class 3205 sits in Platform 1 at night at Winchcombe Station,
Leading Porter Terry Cresswell watches the proceedings.

Right:
GWR 2251 Class no 3205 picks up the light underneath the canopy at Winchcombe.

84

The railway holds two classic transport days each year, and here at Winchcombe Station, standing on the weighbridge which has been refurbished, is the iconic Bedford OB Coach.

Winchcombe Station in the snow a few years ago, is hosting
the railway's Diesel Multiple Unit (DMU).

GWR Pannier no 6412 departs Winchcombe underneath the B4073 roadbridge.

Entering Winchcombe from Cheltenham is one of the stalwarts of the diesel fleet, no 47105.

With the May blossom out on the trees in the cutting, GWR Pannier
no 9681 enters Winchcombe Station with a freight.

Departing past the signals in Winchcombe cutting, still carrying the crosses
to indicate not yet commissioned, is GWR Pannier no 7752.

In Winchcombe cutting, with spring sunshine highlighting the blossom, GWR Prairie no 5542 passes the signals.

An unusual double-header runs through Winchcombe cutting. GWR Hall Class no 6960 "Raveningham Hall" pilots LMS Jubilee no 45596 "Bahamas" on a Gala day.

GWR Heavy Goods Tank Engine no 5224 heads towards the tunnel mouth of Greet Tunnel at the end of the cutting.

Arguably the most famous steam locomotive in the country LNER Class A3 no 4472 "Flying Scotsman" here as BR no 60103 paid a visit to the railway in the early-1990s. She is climbing towards Greet Tunnel.

Above:
GWR 3440 "City of Truro" is at the head of the 'Elegant Excursions'
dining train as she heads into Greet Tunnel.

Left:
GWR Prairie no 5542 climbs towards Greet Tunnel,
photographed from the top of the tunnel mouth.

Blasting out of the north end of Greet Tunnel is visiting engine 'Mickey Mouse' no 46521 pulling a freight train.

GWR Hall Class no 7903 "Foremarke Hall " works hard out of the northern portal of Greet Tunnel with a passenger train.

Another visiting engine LMS 'Mogul' no 2968 is at the head of a freight train as she exits Greet Tunnel heading north.

A summer picture at the northern portal of Greet Tunnel. It is interesting in that the headboard carried by visiting GWR Castle Class no 5051 "Earl Bathurst" is the famous 'Cornishman' and reporting number 675. This West Country train from the Midlands, was usually hauled by a Castle locomotive in BR days and actually travelled down this line in its heyday.

Above:
Looking very smart in its newly-painted blue livery
24081 exits the northern portal of Greet Tunnel.

Right:
Greet Tunnel is the second longest tunnel at 693 yards in preservation,
and here GWR 14XX no 1450 enters the northern portal.

Above:
GWR 14XX no 1450 exits the southern portal of Greet Tunnel with a mixed train.

Left:
At the southern portal of Greet Tunnel GWR Hall Class 7903 "Foremarke Hall" enters with a freight train.

GWR Hall Class no 6960 "Raveningham Hall" brings a passenger train
heading for Cheltenham out of the southern portal of Greet Tunnel.

GWR no 3440 "City of Truro" heads north past the signal operated from
Winchcombe Station signalbox sited at the entrance to the southern portal of Greet Tunnel.

GWR Hall Class 6998 "Burton Agnes Hall" with a freight train heads towards the
southern portal of Greet Tunnel, photographed from the top of the tunnel mouth.

GWR Heavy Goods Tank Engine engine no 4277 starts away from the
signal and heads into the southern portal of Greet Tunnel.

Above:
GWR 28XX no 2857 makes a volcanic exit
from the southern portal of Greet Tunnel.

Right:
LMS 'Mogul' no 2968 heads towards the village of
Gretton with a freight train, Dixton Hill is in the background.

GWR Pannier no 6412 heads towards the hamlet of Stanley Pontlarge on a glorious autumn day.
Stanley Pontlarge was once the home of famous author and preservationist L.T.C. Rolt.

Photographed from the hamlet of Far Stanley, GWR Prairie no 5542 heads toward Gotherington.

Above:
GWR no 3440 "City of Truro" runs through Dixton cutting. A short distance from the
railway is Prescott Hill Climb and the headquarters of the Bugatti Owners Club.

Left:
With primroses flowering on the embankment 9F no 92203
"Black Prince" climbs through Dixton cutting.

GWR Pannier no 9681 works northwards towards Toddington through Dixton cutting.

Visiting GWR Prairie no 4141 passes spring blossom on the embankment of Dixton cutting.

Framed in the trees on the top of the embankment GWR Prairie no 5542 steams
through Dixton cutting northbound. Woolstone Hill can be seen in the distance.

Class 37 diesel locomotive no 37324 "Clydebridge" is also framed in the trees in Dixton cutting.

Bursting through minor roadbridge GWR Hall class no 7903
"Foremarke Hall" enters Dixton cutting northbound.

9F no 92203 "Black Prince" passes under the roadbridge.

Above:
9F no 92203 "Black Prince" is framed in the branches of a tree
as she climbs through the cutting going north.

Left:
Picking up the last of the evening light, GWR Hall class no 6990
"Witherslack Hall" blasts through Dixton cutting northbound.

9F no 92203 "Black Prince" departs from Gotherington Station
and heads for Dixton, Woolstone Hill visible in the background.

GWR Pannier no 9681 steams away from Gotherington Station with the chocolate and cream coach set.

Above:
GWR 14XX no 1450 heads away from Dixton towards Gotherington.

Left:
GWR Pannier no 9681 takes a freight train past the former major product of the Cotswolds. Sheep grazing away as the train passes into Dixton cutting.

9F no 92203 "Black Prince" has been deliberately distressed to recreate the condition of locomotives in the last days of BR steam and looks the part as she heads for Gotherington.

GWR 2251 Class no 3205 exits Gotherington with a mixed train under a dark sky threatening rain.

GWR Hall Class no 7903 "Foremarke Hall" is photographed from Nottingham Hill as she enters Dixton cutting.

Gotherington Station is a private dwelling and the railway has built a halt
on the opposite platform. Here GWR 2251 Class no 3205 pulls away towards Dixton.

9F no 92203 "Black Prince"
blasts through Gotherington
Station on her way north.

GWR 14XX no 1450 pulls
away from Gotherimgton
Halt heading south to
Cheltenham.

An unusual pairing at the 2009 Gala is the Somerset and Dorset 7F no 88 and LNER V2 no 4771 "Green Arrow" with the carmine and cream coaches, as they depart Gotherington, heading south.

This location is called Manor Farm Lane, Gotherington, and GWR Prairie no 5542 heads south around the curve towards Bishops Cleeve.

GER J15 no 65462 hurries through Manor Farm Lane, Gotherington with a freight train.

GER J15 no 65462 and freight train picks up the light as it heads towards Bishops Cleeve.

GWR Hall Class no 7903 "Foremarke Hall" and freight train head away north from Bishops Cleeve.

Picking up the late evening winter light GWR Hall Class 7903 " Foremarke Hall"
and passenger train blast past Manor Farm Lane heading towards Gotherington.

With Cleeve Hill in the background 7903 "Foremarke Hall" heads a train north from Bishops Cleeve.

7903 "Foremarke Hall" picks up the light as shadows play across Cleeve Hill.

9F no 92203 "Black Prince" leaves Bishops Cleeve with the
houses of Southam village on Cleeve Hill in the background.

SR Schools Class 30925 "Cheltenham", actually 30928, takes the first revenue-earning passenger train from the newly opened Cheltenham Race Course Station in 2003, photographed at the bottom of the race course from Southam roadbridge.

SR Schools Class 30925 "Cheltenham" departs the race course, taken at track level.

Whilst the Cheltenham Race Course Station was being renovated and not open to the public a workman's train went down to the station and 4247 is photographed next to the station nameboard.

GWR City class no 3440
"City of Truro" passes the
station nameboard. The
Great Western Railway built
the station just for racegoers
and it was only used on race
days.

SR Schools Class no 30925
"Cheltenham" runs through
the station, which can just
be seen to the left and up
the driveway.

The substantial roadbridge at the south end of Cheltenham Race Course Station carries the major A435.
The line is currently truncated before Hunting Butts Tunnel, and used as a run round.
Here GWR Hall Class 7903 "Foremarke Hall" brings her freight train back into the station.

Also at Toddington Station the North Gloucestershire Railway has its headquarters. This two foot narrow gauge railway
has about half a mile of track and its Toddington Station is adjacent to the the car park. The railways sheds and collections are at
the second station half way along the line, which runs parallel to the standard gauge and terminates at Didbrook.
Here 1906 Arn Jung "Justine" brings a freight train into Toddington Station.

The 1918 Henschel Feldbahn Brigaderlok takes a freight train towards the North Gloucestershire Railway's Toddington Station.

The shape of things to come? The viaduct dwarfing 1450 and auto-trailer coach is Stanway Viaduct to the north of Toddington Station. This 15 arch, 210 yards viaduct will eventually carry trains to Laverton Halt, and ultimately Broadway Station. Track is currently lightly laid to Laverton where a bridge is to be reinstated, and then full steam ahead to Broadway.